Homeland

Mark Willing

Homeland

Homeland
ISBN 978 1 76041 629 4
Copyright © text Mark Willing 2018
Copyright © cover photo Ginninderra Press 2018

First published 2018 by
Ginninderra Press
PO Box 3461 Port Adelaide 5015 Australia
www.ginninderrapress.com.au

Contents

Ethereal City	7
Westgate	8
Spotswood	9
Ascot Vale	10
St Paul's Cathedral	11
Flinders Street	12
Yarra	13
Australia	14
CNN is Down	15
Instagram Lament	16
Signs of the Times	17
Corner Stores	18
Grandmaster	19
Fish Shop	20
A Waitress On Anzac Day	21
Dogs in the Distance	22
Same-sex Marriage	23
Good and Bad Moves	24
Of Mice and Pearls	25
The Meaning of War	26
Jesse's Mountain	27
Dancing Headlights	28
Tentative	29
On Finding a Family Memento of the German Cross	30
Carney	31
Living Without Power	32
Moral Authority	33
Sounds That Are Vanishing	34
The Young Governor	35
An Undertaker's Lament	39

Wild Roses	40
No Password	41
Moment	42
The Faceless	43
Note to Self	44
Extinction	45
Mood	46
The Chemistry of Everything	47
Sighting the Impossible	48
Life Lou, Life	49
Rebellion	50
Zbigniew Herbert's Pebble	52
Memoir – Kew in the Seventies	53
The Business of Risk	54
Future Philosophies	55
A Chip Off the Block	56
CFA	57
The Gentry of Zen	58
Workers Returning	59
Expedition to a Huon Pine	60
Cemetery Autumn	62
Captain of his Soul	63
Poem For Charles Buckmaster	66
Howqua Lullaby	67

Ethereal City

It wears its
own skin well –
reflections behind
glass doors
olfactory reminiscences
through a labyrinth
of alleyways
oily surfaces
coated with bitumen
chrome-plated crypts –

a prickly swab
it spears the glove
into the skin.

Westgate

Iron forearms
a pall of sunlight
cascading from the highest pylon
where briefly it splits
into spectral showers
blinding the unsuspecting
motorist or two
sending shock waves
out over the docklands
a deep throb in the bay
and a marginal ripple
down Sorrento way.
The sun balloons
hot and ashen
as it plummets
behind the monument
decaying in the salt air.

Spotswood

The clean gleam of carriages
at Spotswood station
reminds us of yesteryear.
Yuppies yawn fashionably
treading belatedly into an out-of-date timetable.
Older folk twitch their limbs from the joints
and hang onto steel for security
but the dark sinister masses
surge en masse
spearing black glances
taking up postures
in muscular T-shirts
and tight short skirts
where the centre carriage gyrates
as a Babylon or as a stranger.

Ascot Vale

Showgrounds on a soaking afternoon
after school, taking the train out.
What it's all about and the song 'Alfie'
repeating over and over in your teenage brain
as you enter a miserable new independence
with a dollar-fifty for the experience
minus show bags and rides
but you make up for that
with paper-round money.
Life is a struggle
struggle is a suburb
you've never been to before.
Welcome to Fantasia
the rain never stops.

St Paul's Cathedral

Like any alleyway
the cartels discard
their smaller fry
no one will dine on
nor capitalise from.
The faceless are left
to argue their territory
buttressing bluestone
lanced by the cross
while inside
the holy face of Christ
looks down on tourists
with their flash turned off.
Outside
a whirlwind
of McDonalds wrappers
and empty syringes
seeks solace in the eye of the storm.

Flinders Street

She waits under the clocks
for that uninvited moment
that column of warm air
from which birds of paradise coalesce.
People pass by with electric chatter
their gestures a deft home to somebody –
husband, lover, congenial passenger?
She wills the clocks forward
toward a timeless embrace
or would it be gradual
a few days of coffee and actually conversing
until touch, that on-time express
blurs her world to the end of the line?

Yarra

I come here often.
I watch the ferries
make their way downstream.
I admire the geometries
of the changing skyline
and the flower sellers' commentaries
on what can be seen –
the lovers in arms on the bank lying still
the old men who know and trust only the gulls
the homeless woman whose eye meets mine
who could have been anyone
in my younger days.
Leaving at evening
I would look over her shoulder
at the ferries returning
after another long day
home.

Australia

Put on that earth cardigan that sweater of convict labours that
    slouch hat
that indifference to the time of dreaming
walk out into the city turned to desert
grasp the open fielded air
the shouts of garbage collectors from the street
the painters whistling graffiti onto walls
the mother who hangs old rags from the window ledge
and the drivers who take ring roads around the main idea
walk out but expect no ideal solutions to the broken sewers
the splitting pipes the extravagant joineries the near shanty old
    opulence
nor answers from a god that isn't exactly pulling big crowds
expect nothing know no one except as mate or cobber
bounce off their paid-for emotions like everyone else and laugh
    instead of respond
hold the tallest poppy in your hand while you are led through
    a gallery
of rich ochre prayer or smorgasbords of wider earth
just giggle and burp

but walk out
peep through the crack in your fence
see it
it's called Australia
waiting for you to kneel in the dust
and with handfuls shower
yourself
my people.

CNN is Down

CNN is down.
Ten thousand tweets won't atone.
The left side of the brain is a dire requirement.
Apartments on the right bank yowl from their doors.
Drones above portend the second coming.
Wires cross over from Manhattan to Berlin.
The missile age takes a dim view of the moon.
A million likes for the art of faking.
The coiled rope of erratic reason
knots fivefold in the acrobat's fists.
A tune taps out in a banjo's foot.
The spiritual ape hangs on.

Instagram Lament

I saw you on a cracked screen
of moral anonymity.
I watched as your ideals
accelerated away.
I noticed your skin acquire
the nakedness of transparency
of wings that no longer fly
of demise at the end of a broken chain.
I heard all you said
in the protection of confession.

Unlike all those years ago
when we came upon each other
one on each side of the highway
greeting with a wave and a sign of peace
keeping within a deeper knowing
that lyric pulled out of your hat
then stuffed into a pocket of your swag.
The greeting, the knowing
with no third party
different directions
on the same highway.

Signs of the Times

Tram stop.
Momentary view.
A shop sign fading:
'ANTIQ ARI N BOO SELL RS.'

Under it
a new sign in bright vanilla gloss
'SELF SERVE FROZEN YOGHOURT.'

Corner Stores

Corner conversations, the currency of nations
light up, glance sideways at passing traffic.
Stopovers of crescent or straight-line carriageways
like oases in the middle of suburban thirst.
Recently rotund retirees
milling under neon two-by-two
chatting, discoursing with friendship as benefit
Jack Russell or boxer shadowing their heels.
Opine of philosophy or tucked-in-arm newspaper
or thirtyish housewives showing a new tattoo
here at the meeting place of re-engaged acquaintance
and occasionally, Leo, Ron or Muhammed
exits through rainbow plastic from out back
joining in the fault and gloom of social order.
Flat-white, frothed, Turkish or Methodist
served on one wrought-iron shaky table
with unmatching chairs chocked near horizontal.
Lucidity through sunlight, fresh with a slant
lays truth on the table with prickled opinion.
People of the snap idea, savants of acerbia
quicker-than-wink docos and flash-pan poets.
Inwardly they realise this epic in short time
actually was months, even years in the making
and most of that time, unforeseen preparation
spilled out from these iron and god-wrought mornings.
Old and new residents, one-off passers-by
all stationary in the glow of early dawn brainwaves.
The to-and-fro agreement, the occasional head shake
but always trusted beneath the faded 'open' sign.

Grandmaster

An old man
sitting
under an old vine

playing chess
with himself

grapes
hang
reddening in the evening

raindrops
linger
then drip
from the leaves

his nose
runs
to a tear-like
crystal.

Do you see
God old man
through the vines?

Stalemate.

Fish Shop

I have a blue-collar phone order
docket in hand passed through the heat haze
of the plastic ribboned fish shop.
Truan is carving downpipe on a gyro
with the other hand juggling chips
and between his two selves hiss away
three fillets of an unspecified species
diamond crust adorning their scales
frozen jet squid or barramundi blinged
all the way from Japanese hunting grounds.
A brace of teenagers rides past on BMXs
only to be caught in a web of fathers
standing in guises of patient tradies
who try to explain the communal laws
of riding in populated food zones.
They shimmy off into the large orange sun
taking on peak hour with shock and awe
as Truan, smoothing the butcher's paper
under my nose smiles, flips the basket
and spreads its gold crunch with stout fingers
all the while smiling into my eyes
with a camaraderie of feverish entrapment
sinking low beneath the rim of the steaming sun.

A Waitress On Anzac Day

I serve them
coffee and eggs.

They come in here in suits
with the shine of old medallions

Young men
from older times

Their lapels stained here and there
with shadows they can't explain.

They walk in, big-bodied
their chins tighten and lift

Their mouths straighten high up
and they give me a wink

Of someone who knows
more than he should.

Dogs in the Distance

Like a spark pack-hackled
or a precise lightning strike
or a helicopter hovering
over an accident scene

edgy, out there
pound of heckle or pigskin
discord in the next suburb
distemper of tribes

everything in miniature
everything in distance
until the day of the big one
and it's what the dogs

in the distance
are trying to tell you
it's what they know but cannot say
fearing your fear.

Same-sex Marriage

Strange marriages emerge
up and down our street.
Some water their ornaments
others hose each other down.
Some hide their regard for union
others convey it with petals attached.
Some turn savage in the blink of an eye.
Some hide desire in the eyes of others.
They all retire under the quiet full moon.
They all bury pasts and sink beneath futures
in pockets and arbours fed by the sun –
a random roll call of what fits with what –
melaleuca, geranium, that shiny-leaf thing –
or doesn't. Let the seasons decide.

Good and Bad Moves

I chew the cognac between my teeth
the way I was taught when I was snow-bound
then let it trickle into the warmth of my throat.
The rook cautiously moves
along black and white squares, chuckling
as if it plans to stick around.
From the veranda I watch
a helicopter rattling above
two cars in stretched-out pursuit.
Outmanoeuvring the god of probability
I sip the good with the bad
and pour another hour into safe hands
and listen to the rain beginning
to waken the weary homeless
two doors down and one across.

Of Mice and Pearls

Are we really that real
or are we at most a blind hoax?
Many plantations wilt with starvation
but others grow for the here and now
and within their moonlight gliding
around the powerful owl's bad tidings
that netherworld of mice and pearls
of wise concealment from the all-knowing world
of every rebellion out of sight
in strata high-rise martyred guises
as writers, painters, saints and fighters
those brave and common who dared to dance
knowing deep down they had no chance.

The Meaning of War

A tuppeny clinker
a fiddle-dee bit
his sub nearly sank her
his pants nearly split
tombolas enraged
on the cusp of all out
his sister's engaged
to a guy they call Kraut
a bunkerish heave
on the rock face ashore
where his arms rolled their sleeves
where he couldn't ignore
the boy on the stairs
pressing keys in the sun
skipping corpses for coins
the game's never won.

Jesse's Mountain

i.m. Jesse

The light over the mountain
has tightened into a rain band.
Swart trees will soon diffuse
and the sky will leave the land
and a child, clear to you now
will mount her mare
in the schoolyard paddock
turning for home in time for milking.
Sirens and pedestrian chatter
will all be stripped away
replaced coarsely by a raucous
crowing to arms, to bear down
in a self-correction, a guided turn
a hurdle, city folk may say
but for you, the path
always walked or ridden
along a single ribbon
of upland light.

Dancing Headlights

A moon becomes
a headlight becomes
a sun becomes

Ingamells
three days across the desert
asleep at the wheel
the forgotten and the lost
imagined slithering mirages

turns for home
turns out the lights
the semi ahead
brolga stepping
moon swinging
in its final quadrant.

Tentative

Distilled by a night
of third-world insomnia
Ingamells in the wild territory of the mind
counts the passages of pied currawongs
their withering screams like locomotives
running express past his tent flap
the silhouettes of drowsing huntsmen
sun-shocked on the open weave
as he wistfully strokes the dawn
thinking of spiritual rectitude
the discussion with her the day before
about the kingdom, loss of the mind
the existence in particular smaller than atoms
of the universal spirit. How, beyond
we return to eternity, no
to a timeless sleep
a dot of stationary bliss
in a matrix dotting the sky
like bagatelle
like Ingamells
on the plateau overlooking the dawn
counting screams
in the tentative distance.

On Finding a Family Memento of the German Cross

Somebody waves from the grainy side
in a field somewhere outside Werben.
Shrouded in sepia. The year 1945.
Grammophon is yet to fast forward or rewind.
I return to the carnival of my writing desk
where the whys and wherefores ask why no more.
I wave back through a past half full
taking one-off potshots at the kewpie doll.

Carney

What is so wrong with this balance?
We stir in each other's dreams
an old machine tied up in knots
a strangulation of clown suit collars
a devouring of words, angular and propped
something that is lost before waking.
On a tightwire, our inevitable fate
bounces back and forth
between our bodies.
We are creatures, not thinkers
you and I – we are paid to perform.
In our little caravan at night
I wrap you in dry leaves
to hear you stir in your sleep.
Your head and mine, joined
at the summit, perpetually shrinking
from the world,
its axis of stealth.

Living Without Power

We used to grow vegetables
on the adjacent block of land
our grandfather bought after the war.
We'd cook them on a pot-bellied stove
crackling with logs and bracken
from the clearing at the end of the street.
At night the candles refused to be furious.
They mellowed the ancient tensions of whisky
page turning or knitting ad infinitum.
We slept in ice sheets from dusk to first light
and took our first steps on cold-cracked linoleum.
It was here that structures of first verse were formed
in the need to seek patterns in vapours of warmth.
The melody of magpies and the static of thrushes
invigorated new sounds in our mouths and ears.
It was here the ice of all earth breathed
long after he and his house had gone.
It was here we flared from a smouldering ruin.

Moral Authority

Moral authority: It cannot exist.
Oral suggestions of a distant creed
accord the cord of social growth.
The wait beneath weight of a scoria underworld
where the dead and the corpses no longer fit
grows into this other, this thing that is nameless.
When you go, it will not be you, not I
as useless to believe in unbelief
is the belief we somehow go on
and flesh, carrier of time
fleshless, timeless, bereft of humanness
leaves nothing of yourself to mark your shrine.

Sounds That Are Vanishing

Sounds that are vanishing out of the world
in typewriter heel-clicks, the frights of Luft
my mother's cast-iron forehand lob
at the mahogany wall of the family piano
sustained chord minors and quick treble jabs
long mornings skimming her slowcoach scales
shod clop on cobble, sweet dough aromas
reined irons jangling with bottles of milk
surly ahas in surgical whispers
playground swear words pelted in stone.
There is nothing in the future that cannot be saved
save silence of memory drowned in age
or big-bang bios, fossilised chatter
from stars still to open and speak our names.

The Young Governor

When will it be sir?
When will it be?

You will know boy.
You will know.

Those lumber-sized arms
threading the reefs
thick swollen and sapped
with alchemies of new blood
will come for us
enclose us
with acrid strange forests
and new creatures
you have never seen before.

On your mother's grave boy
your soul will scream
at first for penitence
but gradually subside
and be replaced
by your own curiosity
as it did me
all those journeys ago.
If you're lucky
she might put on
a pretty fair show
pour steam from her belly
and fire from her mouth

she might quake
and your lonely past months
be aborted
by indeed such a seductive prize.

For she's a fair woman boy
she is enough for all
those arms
full mounds
of mountainous ranges
those fingers of viper
swift beckoning
that hair of virulent
waterfalls
those eyes of cruel sun
and scalding sand

you will never forget her
and though you've a home
where your heart will stay
once known, she'll call you
for the rest of your days
and beg promise you will return.

Then over the years
by your children's children
you will alienate then consummate
federate and migrate
populate, violate
democrate and cultivate
and so on and so on
she'll be hauling you in
she'll be spitting you out
with your gut tucked in
and your shirt tails out
as the flag of her adopted doctrine.
Generations will salute your posterior.

And learning to laugh
will be your native tongue
short poppies will adorn
your coat of arms
you'll see through your mirrors
dark faces peering in
she'll coerce you
to say you're sorry.

So boy
take the rudder
we'll sail for such places
unknown on the map of time
yet even now
in the distance
her gales buffet and blow
her perfumes ignite the wind
and we'll be there
in time for history's impasse:

alight lightly
for we have sinned

and you will know boy.
You will know.

An Undertaker's Lament

The pieces haven't fallen yet.
The stars can't match the empty graves.
The edge of town is far from where
you used to ride on saddled wheels.
Your father dug the crying soil
and crafted measure to fit your frame.
The townsfolk heard remains of you
in hymns, in prayer, in silent stress
set stark against the burnished blue
that blew your name, a whispered shriek.
They watched you held at shoulder-height
in aisles of never, nothing more
dots joined in grief from tree to tree
the long-way walk to mark your place.
The stars can't shine on black earth's skin
where sunset reds have all expired
and colour dulled and faded now
will mask the heads still shaking low.
His suit, the one bought by his dad
to start the job in the family name
his patent shoes, dusted red
as all who walk these parts would know
set skyward, pointed outa here
the lonely boring life of stares
of drink-too-much and see-too-little.
The pieces haven't fallen yet.
The stars are lost. They can't shine down.
The father squats and ribs the flame.

Wild Roses

Beneath cliffs of a deadly descent
come the waves, the swell, the ever-chanting heft
of a morose, oceanic lament.
Sensibility lost in turning spirals
and in the chaos, in its spawn
there is stillness in the eye that watches –
a single rose in a maelstrom of storms.

No Password

Death sat pensively
in the chair opposite
and upon the table between them
his hands rummaged for proof.

None of his books would open
no journals, no sheafs
and the password
to all his files
remained locked.

'Google it' he determined.
'Type in anything I've ever said.
Do something.'

But Death sat pensively
then looked at His watch
wiped the table clean
and slapped down an A4,

'You're with me now.
Start again.'

Moment

At that all-defining moment
in the surf at Bondi
riding high on my father's shoulders

facing a wave
larger than houses
its frightening leap
into the corona of sun

at that moment
it seemed a decision
was spawned:

to turn
and let the soft fingers
of silent, slow-motion
disintegration

demolish
laughter
and touch
forever.

The Faceless

The faceless are sweeping
stones from the paths.
Who is coming?
Who will walk there?
A prince? A president?
The stones are ushered
into even rows
in case a stray foot
wanders from the path.
Such exact execution
timed to the moment.
Their flawless heads
turn both ways admiringly.
The path now
as faceless as they.
The visitors will smile.
That's how they like it.
A path without stones
is a people without pride.

Note to Self

You were the mark of Aquarius, the revolt of culture
sitting in the back seat of a hitched ride
your poems secreted in the flap of your duffle coat
and the couple in front, sneering and whispering.

Note to self:
Vote tomorrow. Don't get tattoo.
The tattoo culture has passed me by.
The skin is still willing
but so is the ink
required of a serial poet.

Note to self:
Vote tomorrow. Leave royalties on the fridge.
The hole in the ozone layer is closing.
Is your wall adorned with compounding cc's?
Or did my gypsy-jazz hitchhike
flip the switch making illusion too real?

Note to self:
Don't get ahead of yourself. Breathe.
Your charitable save-the-world treatise
is a stain on everybody's skin.
Life is short. Miracles are scarce. Vote Veto.
Poets get funded less than highways.

Extinction

In the shadow light
of a weightless moon
one orange-bellied parrot
sets out, returns, returns, sets out.
Its head is its heart
a light, weightless organ
designed to search for
unrequited sanctuary.
In this country
it is free
to fill out a census
or not
free to be counted
or not.
Democratic parrots
aleatorically preserved
like orange and yellow correa
that know nothing beyond October.

Mood

On nights like these
it is easy to think
how we had it all.
The warmth of the day lingers
like mellow memory.
The lyrics tuck into you like a first night.

Even the dark surrounding each star
has the glow of a virtuoso.
Even the impossible life they exude
has an arch of mystery down its spine.

The Chemistry of Everything

I watch the tap water
bend around my finger
ignoring the pull of gravity.
Lighter these days
there are photographs I never touch
or look at. There is no memory.
At night I hear the helicopter
perusing the rooftops along my street
and I remain oblivious
through my wasted portals
to anyone who might glance in.
I touch the water like a skin
that once caught me hopelessly unaware
that taught me all the knots of love
proving above all secrecy and fact
that light bends. There is no illusion.

Sighting the Impossible

The comfort-zone warranty
of the soul
lies deep, entrenched
within the core

as midpoint of a V formation
hexagonal bone of honey
or an ocean in a canine eye

embedded like
a planetary dervish
still-point of a spurious moon

sway of focal token
outside of the flesh
and looking in
searching for its fine print.

Life Lou, Life

I want to put my copy
of *Howl* away because
I need order within my revolution.
But I miss Lou Reed
not just in flesh
but his incisive riffs
and dark monologues
and his mystery companions.
I used to dream
as I listened that
I was walking in
on an already-evolved
jam or melodic motif
and that long after I had gone
they would still be jamming
(is that how you see it, Lou?)
I guess that's life.
We enter and leave
and the show goes on.

Rebellion

he got it
'just desserts' a metro junkie screamed

'they all scream' whispered the east European woman
on the seat next to me.

someone uttered the correction 'just deserts'

the junkie screamed again 'whatever' 'he was just a kid'
and burst into tears

'how'd he get over there' one construction worker asked
'where were his parents'

another wanted to know when he learned to drive a truck

'I think it was a van' the priest in the corner corrected

'cmon, cmon,' said the junkie standing in the doorway
'you're missing the point he was going there
to get away from all yous
what you sell us, what you buy
to keep us quiet, all the lies
he was only rebelling'

'when I was rebelling back in my day' started the chippy
'I pinched me dad's ute for a night
or got drunk in the local park
I didn't go blowin people up in the middle east'

'I started smoking' said the secretary
'I put money on the horses' said the soldier
'I joined the army' said the cat burglar
'I wrote and performed folk songs at festivals' said Lin Li

the young kid in the doorway shook his head in disgust
'you don't get it do ya'
he opened the door and stepped onto the platform
he stepped out and walked away
he walked out and stepped away.

Zbigniew Herbert's Pebble

The calm, clear eye
of Herbert's pebble
is all I crave.

Transient, transparent
it must be a discovery
in a lucid state

that is not water
not vapour, not earth.
It will speak

of centuries of fire
and of ice.
It is formed this way

for the preservation
of a face or a hand
in rippling absentia.

Memoir – Kew in the Seventies

Whiteness of walls – everywhere
in the heritage of memory that stays

that time when walls, agelessly
lived with, but did not hold us

when we were free to look outward
from our rendered balcony, and the world was good.

Now not so much a stucco aggregate
as a tended heart, growing wild in our memories

indoor pastimes in Prussian order
of poem first, then poem, like Tenebrae's

soaring angels, our ceiling of poltergeists
we would laugh at till dawn, eye-level Art

Nouveau over the wealthy and the poor.
I would not expect you now to hear me

but hands occasionally touch, overshadow.

The Business of Risk

Sometimes
he would surprise himself
in the small hours
watching his ghostly shadow
writing something he was not privy to.
Then, before sleep arrived
peeling it from the wall
alongside his writing table
he would find only
a blank sheet
with a note attached:
'Be Back Soon.'

Future Philosophies

Synthesised leaf spur
thickening with hours.
Its dense matriculation
into succulent girth
knowing in another time
it will most likely form
another apposite branch
of unknowable knowledge.

A Chip Off the Block

When Baghdad was taken
the statue stood obliquely erect
to the point of being obliquely disrespected.

It was streamed, beamed live
and replay replayed
more often than a moon landing –
icon of that time
curtailing terror, entering unknowns
saying boo to a goose round every corner.

That single lean a permanent image
a thousand times more than the error of Pisa
of might, of indestructible right
the journey of democratic goodness, no blight
upon the name of Allah or Christ.

When they came to dismantling
the streamings ceased
and programming returned to a man named Brady
but somewhere in alley dust
a small hand planted
a chunk of the right arm
still waving still.

CFA

Every day they live on a map
of incidents and warnings.
They don't eat for up to
fourteen hours at a time.
Their instinctual hunger
lies in turning toward the fight.
Their arms push only forward.
They know no other way.
They often speak of the Big One of 39
or the sneaky one of 83.
09 sticks in the craw
and is never spoken of
except in whispers
but even there disjoints itself
from human reality.
They toss another snag
and laugh over a beer about
politics, partners, work
but never God.
They leave that chat
to the wrath and pall
crowning the top of the distant hill.

The Gentry of Zen

The first thing that strikes you
is the gentry of Zen
warm embraces and secret handshakes
a brotherhood.

The next is defences totally down
the mantis slide
ascending palms to the air.
Relatives watch from the side

and you can't help but feel
a floating immersion
of flesh and emotion, expressed
by block and by parry

then the slow hiss of release
knowing all things return –
the bow then stillness
of values preserved.

Workers Returning

Vests with the smell of hay
over shirts hardly washed
over a skin of dark sweat
over a chest and a heart
over something
restored

the streaky yellows
the puffed-up reds
writhe into an elegant
orange sky

returning
from fields
into the smoky
reunions
of their whispered
hallelujahs
and amens.

Expedition to a Huon Pine

What are the forces that bring us here?
Are they hidden in this tubular vault
or in the extinct ghosts of absurd longevity?
Destiny and density of impassable bush
remain at odds with each other.
Past this tree and that – so many names
and so many reasons for not entering.
Days slow into years, then millennia
until true to its honesty, our host appears.
At once, only awe fills our vocabulary.
Like children dancing around a flame
we circle our arms around its impossible girth
so many limbs, long-since dead
lie stacked about the root-line
like the breadth of history
too wide to be measured
too old for reasons
its sap dissolved into three thousand years.

To think, he cared not
for all the accessions to power
for Waterloo or for Rome
nor empires, nor Buddha, nor Christ
not even the Genesis chronicles.
Not even recounts of these stirred his leaves.
Only the air of this wilderness forest
completed his necessary picture of life.
What force still surrounds us
as we rub our hands across him?
There are those who act and those who speak.
There are things many times over
that in their majesty
exist.

Cemetery Autumn

There are, inside of you always
the footsteps beside the cemetery wall.
There are autumn leaves everywhere
waded through, wrapped by April winds
stirring around your legs
making light journey, a hand with roses
to the lamp of your love
in an upstairs kitchen.
The dark as always
descends damp and early
and the leaves in the cemetery
have come and gone once more
their aching cold, always
over years, inside of you.

Captain of his Soul

Speak no more of afterlife. It exists
Speak only of death. It does not

*

As much as I loved you in this place
it is not here anymore that I can breathe

the air, or your scent well-meaning

*

Surfaces of the artery
blossoming in the water garden

contained in your eyes
your vision, your world

*

A tree of hands overlooks your life
we hear your footprint on the burnt

summer grasses

*

In a harbour of moonlight
we take water bottles and tea

you never complained, your stars always shone
you wanted it that way in the fluorescence of passage

*

Mysterious the dark behind the door
in joyous sunlight I sometimes make out

a movement in that other world

*

Two bolts fallen from the shelf
to the now empty floor where you slept

so many travesties of inertia now
beneath your brilliant ethereal touch

*

You say I should get on with my life
run the fantastic gauntlet of days

but part of me always returns
to the shade of your perpetual vine

*

Stone and grass, the flat spaces
our personas spread out upon

each yielding talk of that other voice
the footstep, the silent shoot

*

Within this cloak of separation
we regale the sun
in the moment we waken from your dream

regale the sun to bear
to continue your conversation
regain the morning, it exists.

Poem For Charles Buckmaster

yr chisel-jawed
reconciliation
with the valleys and peaks
with lostness
with poetry
with family
comes thru
every year
with the news
of yr passing
and we wait
knowing and feeling
that going down
of desire
when the heart bleeds
in its own cavity

but it's the ones like you
that keep us going
that keep the sea
and the land
and the horizon sky
from melting
into one.

Howqua Lullaby

1

Do you remember
the pink orchid when we moved here
that burnt and dry December?

I wouldn't let you touch it.
Three days and nights with little sleep
a place with no name, no epithet.

The valley corsets inward on both sides
the wind sucks oxygen from its porous wings.
Another dimension is required

for you and I
explorers on the great verge
of resemblances of you and I.

2

Old Stoney saved four houses last night
the owners long fled
with empty utes, quick goodbyes.

Two nights earlier
the three of us joined forces
with high range jets of water

propelled from pumping volleys
to fight back the front
and save the valley

3

Too old for this we sit
and wait on the rocky steppe
the orchid aflame and sunlit

watching old Stoney's fountains shooting
into the flaming heart over and over
up in the distance with a northerly whipping

mirboo into frenzied swarms
our own pumps idling around us
barely heard over the oncoming storm.

Deckchairs, leathers, the occasional newspaper
and a radio crackling a sombre song
reduced to a frail inaudible wafer.

4

Do you know me still
in that other space
humanless and god-filled

as you murmur
in fitful excuses for sleep
with dream's black humour

does my hand touch yours
or do you dream it
as moving, ghostly fingers

of smoke
rise up
to your throat?

5

Do you remember the pale pink orchid
you carried in the front seat
of our ute, never leaving it

to trust the strength
of my palm –
did you know me then?

6

Funnels of already dead dry leaves
twigs, even small branches
drag and weave

toward you where you lie
closer now
I dream to be fire

so I clamber the way
a body pulls itself
into another's resting shape

to cover and pass through
the other
to become one anew

but your arms fight me
like the invisible cortex of immolation
hanging itself from the highest trees

like ever-changing batwing
fending off its own searing skin
scorched and writhing

their red lining
sheeting into furious ascension
unfolding and finally, unending.

7

Does the touch
of hell warm or blister
as much

as your pink hand
your calloused trust
can understand

the years and stagnation
of touch
without violation?

8

Solitude is a runaway horse
bridled to that other
slouched over its back, brought

riding into town
with the smell of burnt flesh
of forbidden flowers

9

Over your shoulder the narrow valley
rises in flame and palls of nightmare.
You stir, but your eyes are empty.

Black silhouettes of shimmering limbs
exploding plumes of dust-grey chlorophyll
surround the quivering tangle where I cover him

10

Your hand smears my forehead
as we watch the snaking dilapidation
of the valley up ahead

your hand the one constant
extinguishing my deepest fear
cold, almost non-existent

your hand of the twenty thousand nights
grafted in black ruin
itself to my orchid's pure delight

the prickly rush of desensitised skin
acknowledging but not seeing
its own numbness, its kin

this sticky friction of painful warmth
human-tempered unlike charcoal
in which some spirit may still be stored

11

A final cremation, your last stroke
smears across my forehead
then slows

as if to blacken
all memory and rise up
then beckon

to swallow us now
in one cobra strike.
Our orchid bows.

12

The valley has become a narrow, blood-red stalk
bleeding blue flame of wraith stick figures
zigzagging toward us against all laws

Who we've become is a marriage of stone
caves in on itself
and implodes.

Slowly I touch a numbness of charcoal
a mortality of trees, a retreating storm
a portrait of embers no face can hold.

Is this how we pray
beaten down by elements
into a single atom or phrase

for what is this ampersand –
marriage? –
Is it all we have left to inherit and understand?

As the past erupts into tongues of sharp precipice
and your words the brittle spit
of a final defiance…

www.ingramcontent.com/pod-product-compliance
Lightning Source LLC
Chambersburg PA
CBHW062152100526
44589CB00014B/1795